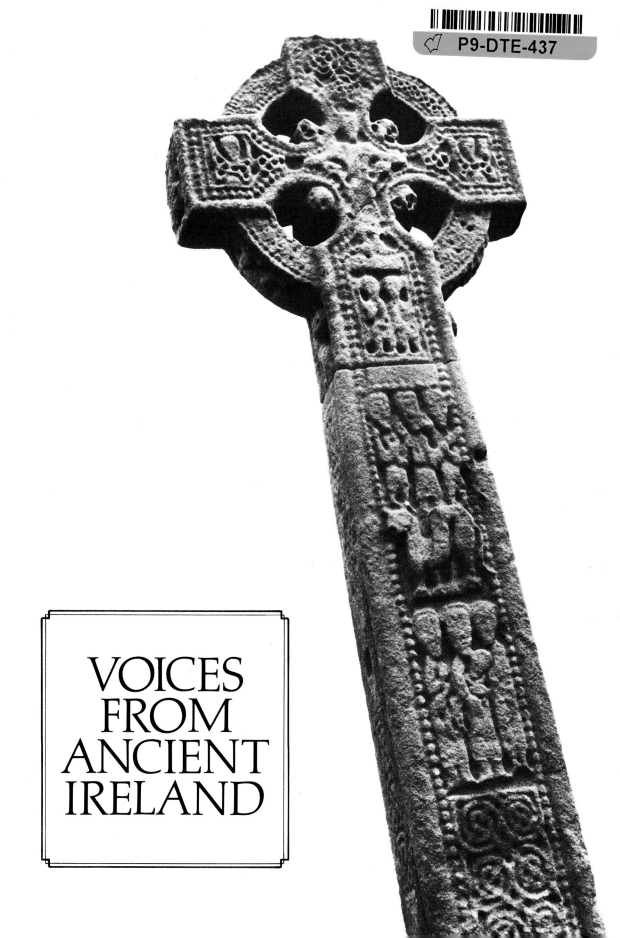

VOICES FROM ANCIENT IRELAND

VOICES
FROM
ANCIENT
IRELAND

A BOOK OF EARLY IRISH POETRY

Photographs and English translation by

BOB WILLOUGHBY

Irish Adviser: John Caball

Pan Original
Pan Books London and Sydney

First published 1981 by Pan Books Ltd,
Cavaye Place, London SW10 9PG
© Bob Willoughby 1981
ISBN 0·330 26274 2
Printed and bound in Great Britain by
Fakenham Press Limited, Fakenham, Norfolk.

Contents

'Pleasant indeed this hill of Howth'

12th century?
Attributed to St Columcille – saying farewell to his beloved
Ireland, banished for his sins to Scotland's island of Iona.

'What pleasure to be enclosed on an island'

12th century
Both of these poems are from manuscripts several centuries
after St Columcille's death, revealing how strong his impact
was on the poets and clergy of the time.

'Sad this life'

12th century
From *The Frenzy of Suibhne Geilt* [*Mad Sweeney*] – the saga of a
7th century prince driven mad during the battle of Magh Rath.
Cursed by a cleric he had insulted, he was doomed to wander
the forest as a hermit, seeking his peace.

'Cold this night in Moin Mohr'

8th/9th century

'Young stag, little belling one'

12th century
From *The Frenzy of Suibhne*, stanzas 1–12.

'When I am among the old ones'

9th/10th century

'The wee bird'

9th century

'Fruitful glen of fish-filled pools'

14th century
From *Deirdre remembers a glen*.

Additional Notes

Introduction

When I first read some of these early Irish nature poems, I was amazed at just how rich the imagery was, and the clarity of the vision of the early monks and poets. Describing their world with a morning-fresh eye, that especially appealed to me as a photographer.

In casting about for more material, I found no end of books, all basically directed for the student interested in Celtic studies. Very little was available for one just to sit down and read for the pleasure of it.

Like all converts I wanted to share this new discovery with my friends. However there just weren't any books one could find as an appropriate gift.

This set me off compiling my favourites, learning to read the Irish letters and dictionaries, working with friend and expert in the Irish, John Caball. Two years later, the new English versions of the original Irish are what you find in this volume, and in its companion, *My Irish Love* – love poems of some few hundred years later when the influence of France and 'courtly love' was abroad in Ireland.

These poems, just a few of many, reveal an innocence, a love of beauty, and simplicity rarely found in any other body of literature, a glimmer of another era. If you listen you'll be able to hear the *Voices from Ancient Ireland*.

BOB WILLOUGHBY

May-day, season fair,
perfect time of year,
the blackbird's song a poem
to the sun's first slender ray.

The constant cuckoo calls
to delightful summer;
end of the bitter weather
that pierced the branching wood.

Summer cuts small the stream,
swift horses seek the water,
heather spreads its long hair,
delicate cotton-grass prospers.

The hawthorn buds forth,
the peaceful flow of the sea
puts the ocean to sleep.
Blossom covers the world.

Bees of small strength carry
the flower-harvest with their feet;
the cattle bring to the mountain
a rich-pouring abundance.

The music of the trees,
a melody providing perfect peace;
dust is blown from the dwelling places,
haze on a lake of full waters.

The corncrakes' chorus,
the high pure waterfall singing
welcome in the warm water,
rustling rushes reply.

Swallows dart to heaven,
mysterious music surrounds the hill,
the forest fruit grows fair and fat,
the swamp, silently sounding.

Bog, black as the raven's coat,
strident the bold cuckoo,
the trout leaps,
the warrior strong and vigorous of limb.

Man's power increases,
swiftly gaining fresh vitality;
every wood pleasing to see,
every plain as beautiful.

Pleasant this time of year,
gone, winter's fury;
forest bright, pasture fruitful,
summer joyous, peace immense.

A flock of birds settle
where a woman works the land;
the murmuring in a green field
of a bright swift stream.

Excitement in the fierce riding of horses
scattering the ranks of men;
the prospering pond
turns the iris to gold.

Timid, the man afraid to speak,
the bold, sings confidently;
rightly does he proclaim,
May-day, fairest season!

9th century

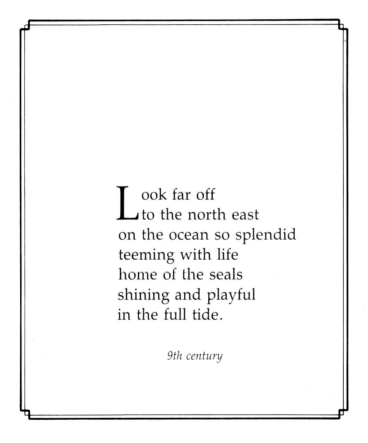

L ook far off
to the north east
on the ocean so splendid
teeming with life
home of the seals
shining and playful
in the full tide.

9th century

Such scandal, my thoughts
how they slip away,
I dread the woe to come
reaped on Judgement Day.

Across the psalms they go
on paths not right
they run, they shout, they dance
under the very eye of God.

Through crowded assemblies,
through groups of giggling girls,
through woods, through towns
faster than the wind.

They take the path of virtue
at times without a doubt,
then off again on wicked ways
they're just as sure to go.

They start off with evil steps,
without boat cross every sea,
with only one quick leap, jump
from earth to heaven.

They run but not a race too wise,
bounding here and there,
after voyages indiscreet
return home to me.

Though one tries to bind them
by fettering their feet
they never wish to settle,
they do not care to sleep.

The sound of whipping
seems not to slow their flight,
like the tail of an eel
they slip through my grasp.

Firm lock nor vaulted cell
nor any chain or bond,
fort nor sea nor dungeon bare
can halt their run.

O truly chaste and gentle Christ,
my every thought you clearly see,
may the Spirit of the seven graces
keep them, restrain them.

Rule my heart
O Creator just,
that I may have your blessing,
that I may do your will.

O Christ, give me your love
that we may be as one,
you are infinite, not subject to weakness
as I am.

10th century

O contented blackbird
nesting where you please,
hermit who rings no bell,
sweet soft peaceful your call.

11/12th century

The forest's wall surrounds me,
sweet praise for the blackbird's song.
Above my copy book
the birds in chorus!

High above
the grey-headed cuckoo sings to me
God's promise . . . may He protect me
writing well beneath the wood.

8th/9th century

Alone in my small cell,
	peace for company,
blessed retreat
before meeting with death.

A hidden secluded dwelling,
praying for forgiveness,
a conscience unafraid
directed towards heaven.

A body pure, of good habits,
stamping on it manfully,
eyes downcast and tearful
for the subduing of my passions.

Passions weakened and withered
in renunciation of this world,
pure ardent thoughts
seeking pardon from God.

Prayers from my heart
towards cloudy heaven,
earnest and devout confession,
fervent showers of tears.

A very cold bed, fearful
like the sleep of a doomed man,
sleep short and restless,
invocations frequent and early.

My food, my ration,
my prayerful restraint
will not make me sinful
from eating.

A measure of dry bread,
head bowed in thanksgiving,
water from a pleasant slope
that is all one could ask.

A bitter meagre diet,
thoughtful attention to one's book,
a hand stayed from quarreling and visiting,
a calm easy conscience.

Blessed sight to see
the saints pure of soul,
thin emaciated cheeks,
skin weathered and lean.

Christ the son of God come to me,
my Creator my King,
my spirit seeks Him
in the kingdom where He is.

Let this place shelter me,
these holy walls,
a spot beautiful and sacred
and I there alone.

8th/9th century

To go to Rome
great the effort, little the gain,
you will not find there the King you seek
unless you bring Him with you.

9th century

Arran of the many deer,
  sea touching against her shoulder,
island of the pleasing gaps,
her ridges rich green in the golden rays.

High over the sea her summit,
sweet her herbs, rare her swamps,
green island of glens filled with horses,
blessed land to the people of the groves.

Reckless the hind upon her peaks,
tender bogberries in her thickets,
cool the water in her rivers,
acorns on her brown oaks.

Keen-eyed her hares and hounds,
blackberries and fruit of the dark blackthorn
weaving their wall in the woods,
wretched the trees in the contending.

The rocks collecting purple cover,
grass flourishing on her slopes,
the protecting crags conceal
leaping fawn, bounding bucks.

Smooth her plain, fat her swine,
pleasant her crops, (true indeed),
nuts on the tips of the hazel woods,
the long ships go sailing past.

Delightful when fair weather comes,
trout under the brinks of her rivers,
seagulls call around her white cliffs,
delightful at all times is Arran!

12th century

No pleasure
for me
tormenting the one I love.

Only fear
of God's fury
kept me from his desire.

Denying him
caused the pain,
yet heaven's not easily won.

This then
turned Cuirithir against me,
a small thing compared to my love.

Liadan I,
who loved Cuirithir so,
true as anything can be.

Too fleeting
that quiet time
alone with Cuirithir.

The forest
would sing to us
blending with the sounds of the mighty sea.

My wish
for Cuirithir to understand
these things that keep us apart.

Hiding nothing
were I to love all men
he would still be my heart's desire.

My heart
broken and aflame,
without him it has no life.

9th century

Sweet bell
struck on a stormy night,
better for me going to that meeting
than along with a foolish woman.

9th century

Astory to tell,
    the stag sings
of winter snow
of summer past.

High cold wind,
the sun sits low
brief its journey,
seas swiftly flow.

Ferns redden
losing shape;
wild geese make
familiar cries.

Cold grips
the wings of birds,
icy season . . .
that's all to tell.

9th century

Pleasant indeed this hill of Howth,
high over the white-breaking sea,
proud hill of the many ships,
vine-growing, eager, warlike peak.

Peak where Fionn and the Fianna stood,
that once boasted the riches of kings,
where brave Dairmuid brought
Grainne one day, in bold flight.

Most beautiful peak of all Ireland
lording high over a sea of gulls;
leaving it a heartbreaking step,
radiant peak of the ancients.

Great the speed of my curragh
its stern towards Derry,
penance for me to travel by sea
to Scotland's edge.

There is a grey eye
which will look back upon Erin,
never will it see again
the men of Ireland or her women.

St Columcille's Farewell
12th century?

What pleasure to be enclosed on an island
      high on a rock
where I may reflect on the sea
in all its moods.

Where I may see the great waves
shining bright and cheerful
singing music to their Father
on their perpetual course.

That I may see the even bright-edged strand
no gloomy view,
that I may hear the song of the wonderful birds
a joyous prayer.

That I may hear the crash of the mighty waves
against the rock,
the roar of the sea
crying out near the churchyard.

That I may watch the soaring flocks of birds
over the fullness of the sea,
that I might see its mighty whales
greatest of wonders.

That I might watch the ebb and tide
and on its course, that it may take
my name and the secret that I whisper
back to Ireland.

That contrition of heart would come to me
in contemplation,
that I may lament my sins
so difficult to declare.

That I may bless the Creator
who rules all things,
heaven with its pure order of angels,
earth, sea, everything.

That I may meditate with one of my books
for the good of my soul,
a while at adoration of beloved heaven,
a while at psalms.

A while gathering seaweed from the rocks,
a while fishing,
a while giving food to the poor,
a while in my cell.

Time to pray for the kingdom of heaven,
for our salvation . . .
a labour not too hard!
that would be pleasant.

St Columcille
12th century

Sad this life
no place of rest,
a house of cold frost
and harsh driven snow.

Icy wind,
faint shadow of sun,
shelter of a single tree
atop this barren height.

Suffering the rain
following deer paths
across green meadows,
morning of shining frost.

The Frenzy of Suibhne
12th century

Cold this night in Moin Mohr,
the lashing rain,
the freshening wind's voice
thunders over the sheltered wood.

8th/9th century

Young stag, little belling one
the sound of your voice
is sweet to us
echoing in the glen.

A longing for my tiny house
has filled my heart,
the fox in the plain,
the deer in the mountain.

Oak so grand, so full-leafed,
rising high above the trees,
hazel bush, sweet branching one
fragrant your store of nuts.

Alder my friend
fine in your colour,
your thorns are not sharp to me
in the gap where you grow.

Blackthorn, you proud prickly
dark plum bearer,
watercress, green-topped cluster
at the edge of the blackbird's well.

Saxifrage of the pathways,
sweetest of all the herbs,
green, very green one
of the wild strawberries.

Apple tree, fruitful apple
roughly do men shake you,
rowan tree, dear rowan tree
beautiful your blossom.

Briar, sharp spiny tooth
you do not grant fair terms,
you never cease to tear me
until you've your fill of blood.

Yew tree, gentle yew
familiar to churchyards,
ivy, peaceful
invader of the dark woods.

Holly, sheltering one,
door against the wind,
ash tree, deadly weapon
in the hands of the warrior.

Birch, smooth and blessed,
proud and melodious,
beautiful the tracery of your branches
reaching to your crest.

Aspen tree that tremble so,
hearing at times
the fluttering of your leaves,
I think it is the foray!

The Frenzy of Suibhne 1–12
12th century

W hen I am among the old ones
I am a reminder that games are forbidden,
when I am among the wild youth
they think that I am younger.

9th/10th century

The wee bird
whistles welcome
with a bill bright
yellow.

Crystal clear call
over lovely Loch Laig
blackbird in a bush
yellow bright.

9th century

Fruitful glen of fish-filled pools
  beautiful your rounded hills of wheat;
remembering you causes me great distress,
glen of bees and the horned wild ox.

Glen filled with cuckoo, thrush and blackbird,
joyous forest to every fox,
glen of garlic, green with cress,
flowering clover curly-crested.

The clear voice of the red-backed deer
under the oak tree, high on the summit
gentle hinds and they so timid
lying hidden in your well-wooded glade.

Glen of the scarlet-berried rowan
fruit praised by every flock of birds,
for the badgers a sleepy seclusion
quiet in their burrows with their young.

Glen of the silent blue-eyed hawk
glen with rich bounty from every tree
glen sheltered by peaks on every side
glen of the blackberry, wild plum and apple.

Glen of the sleek brown flat-nosed otter
leaping lightly, freely fishing,
many are the graceful white-winged swans,
salmon spawning in the stony streams.

Glen of the tangled branching yew
glen of mists and gentle cows
glen of the clear brilliant sun
glen of the graceful women, perfect as pearls.

Deirdre remembers a glen
14th century

Additional Notes

The poet in Ireland was held in very special respect from the beginning. Bishop, king and chief poet all had equal status.

However, to become a poet meant a rigorous apprenticeship of up to twelve years. The poet was required to know at least 350 classic narratives, some lasting for hours, to memorize genealogies, and topographical traditions, beside coping with the hundreds of complex metres and disciplines that would boggle the mind today.

Their poetry has such style, and is so sophisticated in a form rich with alliteration and assonance, internal rhymes and metre, that it can never properly be translated into another language.

Consequently I have concentrated mainly on the content, preserving as much form and alliteration as possible, but never at the expense of the original text, or sacrificing the meaning in any way.

The poets, when at their height, travelled from castle to castle, often with huge retinues. The rewards were great. The lords of the manor or castle, intimidated by the satire the poets might write about them, were literally afraid to refuse them anything.

This eventually led to such excesses by the poets that the kings banded together and threatened to banish them all. Even the intercession of St Columcille, brought dramatically back from his monastery in Iona, failed to save the day for them. They eventually did die out for various reasons, but not without a broadside of poems marking their demise, and an end to a great era.

The oral tradition still lives in the speech of the Irish today – the lyric way they organize names and places and dates into their everyday speech. The pleasure of the words and the pleasure of the sound of words create the character of the Irish conversation. 'The language for your prayers, your curses, and your love making', reflects this ancient continuity.

The poems represented in this book are often from a number of different manuscripts of the same poem and pieced together. 'May-day', which opens this collection, is one of those 'difficult' ones, with many corrupted lines. What is there is too good to omit, however.

The great Celtic scholars who have made any collection of Irish poetry possible must be given a very grateful credit. Their years of research, in uncovering the ancient manuscripts and creating the corpus that everyone now may so freely draw from, can never be repaid: Kuno Meyer, Robin Flower, Gerard Murphy, Kenneth Jackson, Eleanor Knott, Myles Dillon, T. F. O'Rahilly, Daniel Corkery, to name but a few.

Today poet-scholars such as Sean O'Tuama and John Montague still pursue that all-too-elusive Irish Muse, and in their encouragement of the student in Celtic studies we are ensured that in years to come we shall continue to hear the *Voices from Ancient Ireland*.

Bob Willoughby
Coolmaine Castle
Co. Cork, Ireland